BEST BIBLE STORIES

The Boy Who Ran Away

THE BOY WHO RAN AWAY

Jennifer Rees Larcombe

Illustrated by Steve Björkman

CROSSWAY BOOKS • WHEATON, ILLINOIS
A DIVISION OF GOOD NEWS PUBLISHERS

The Boy Who Ran Away
Text copyright © 1992, 1997 by Jennifer Rees Larcombe
Illustrations copyright © 1997 by Steve Björkman
U. S. edition published 1999 by Crossway Books
a division of Good News Publishers
1300 Crescent Street
Wheaton, Illinois 60187
First British edition published 1992
by Marshall Pickering as part of *Children's Bible Story Book.*
This book published as a separate edition in 1997
by Marshall Pickering, an Imprint of HarperCollins Religious,
part of HarperCollins Publishers,
77-85 Fulham Palace Road, London W6 8JB.
Cover design: Cindy Kiple
First U. S. printing 1999
Printed in Hong Kong
ISBN 1-58134-053-2

THE BOY WHO RAN AWAY

John 7:12; Luke 15:1–2, 11–24

Jerusalem was full of whispers. When Jesus arrived for the feast that year, everyone seemed to be staring at Him.

"He's a good man," said some people.

"No!" others replied. "He says He's God,

so He must be a liar."

"Just look at Him now!" exclaimed the Pharisees in horror when they saw Jesus sitting in a back street surrounded by most of the city's robbers, murderers and bad women.

"If He was really God, He certainly wouldn't go near people like that," they

sniffed. But when they heard what Jesus was saying they were even more angry.

There was once a farmer who had two sons. "I wish I lived in the city," the younger boy was always thinking. "I'd go to

parties every night and

eat and **drink** till morning.

I'm **sick** of this **boring** farm."

In the end he asked his father for his share of the
family money and off he went.

A big house and cool clothes soon bought him

lots of friends, but they only

liked him because he gave them presents and asked them to his parties.

One terrible day he realized that he had wasted
all of his money. "Never mind," he thought.
"My friends will look after me."

But they didn't want to
be his friends anymore,
now that he was poor.
No one in the whole
city would give him a
job, so in the end he
wandered out to the
country.

"You can look after my pigs," said a farmer, but he was so mean he gave the boy nothing to eat.

The pigs smelled awful, and the rotting garbage they ate was even worse, but he was so hungry he scooped it up from the muddy ground and began to eat.

"Why did I ever leave my father?" he sobbed. "HE would never treat his servants like this. They're all well fed and warmly dressed."

Suddenly, he jumped to his feet. "That's what I'll do," he exclaimed. "I'll go home and tell my father how sorry I am. Perhaps he'll let me work as his servant."

All those people in that back street knew just how the boy in the story must have felt. "Would the father turn his son away?" they wondered as they listened eagerly.

When the boy was still a long way from home his father saw him, because he had been watching for his son all the time he was away. He **ran** down the road with his **arms open wide,** and the thin, ragged boy stumbled towards him.

"Father, I'm sorry,"

he cried as his father kissed him.

"Come on," smiled the father. "Let's get you into some clean clothes. Tonight we'll have a feast to welcome you back." Putting his arm around the boy, they walked home together.

A great sigh of relief went round the crowd.
Surely Jesus was telling them that

God would

forgive them

too, however bad

they were, if only
they would ask Him.

Let's talk about the story

1. Why did the young boy want to go to the city?

2. Were the people in the city really his friends?

3. What made the boy want to go home? What happened when he got there?

4. Why did Jesus tell this story?

5. Have you ever done anything that made you feel far away from God?

6. It's important to apologize to God and anybody that we have hurt or done something wrong to. Do you need to apologize and ask forgiveness of somebody?